Flying Scotsman

Flying Scotsman

ALAN PEGLER
CECIL J. ALLEN
TREVOR BAILEY

LONDON

First printed 1969

SBN 7110 0107 3

Published by Ian Allan Ltd, Shepperton, Surrey
Printed in Great Britain

Introduction

"Flying Scotsman": what thoughts that magical name conjures up. It was the Flying Scotsman that was always featured in children's picture books of our youth, the crack high speed express of the East Coast railway route between London and Edinburgh via York; it was the Flying Scotsman that took us to Scotland for holidays; and at times the Flying Scotsman has included a cinema coach and hairdressing saloon. Yet what is the Flying Scotsman? No one knows quite when the name was coined, for the 10 am expresses from Kings Cross and Edinburgh were known by the nickname "Flying Scotsman" long before the title was officially bestowed on these trains in 1927. Four years before, however, the name *Flying Scotsman* was given to the third of Gresley's newly-built Class A1 Pacifics, then No. 1472, but soon renumbered as 4472 under the LNER renumbering scheme of that time. Thus was born what has become, without doubt, the most famous locomotive in the world. It was the engine chosen by the LNER to represent the best in locomotive design at the Wembley Exhibition in 1924; it was the engine which worked the first regular non-stop run of the 10 am "Flying Scotsman" express in 1928, and in 1934 it achieved Britain's first officially authenticated 100 mph maximum down Stoke Bank on a test run.

There were, it is true, more praiseworthy exploits by other locomotives; *Coronation*'s 114 mph in 1937 and *Mallard*'s 126 mph in 1938—the world record for steam traction—yet somehow it was the locomotive *Flying Scotsman* which captured public imagination, even after it had been replaced by more modern forms of motive power on crack expresses and despite losing its historic number, 4472, to become No. 103 and, later, British Railways 60103. When the locomotive was scheduled for withdrawal by British Railways, Alan Pegler, in buying *Flying Scotsman* and restoring it to its well-known LNER apple green livery with its original number of 4472, won the thanks of millions, for *Flying Scotsman* alone represents the last of the steam age on British Railways; it is the only one of the many preserved locomotives that is allowed to run on BR main lines today and which it will do until the agreement between Alan Pegler and the BRB expires in 1971. During 1969 *Flying Scotsman* is to add another honour to its credit for it is to cross the Atlantic to haul a British trade exhibition tour train in the United States of America.

This book tells the story of 4472 through the writing of historian Cecil J. Allen who surveys East Coast motive power in general, and *Flying Scotsman* in particular, Alan Pegler—No. 4472's owner—who describes what life is like with an express locomotive as part of the family, and Trevor Bailey, who recalls the 40th anniversary of the non-stop run to Edinburgh in May 1968. Finally, an album section is devoted to photographs of 4472 in action from the cameras of some of Britain's finest railway photographers.

The Flying Scotsman Story

CECIL J. ALLEN

ON JUNE 1, 1862, there started simultaneously at 10 o'clock in the morning from Kings Cross terminus in London and the Waverley Station, Edinburgh, two trains which eventually were to become famous the world over. At first the pair were described in the timetables of the Great Northern, North Eastern and North British Railways—the three partners in the East Coast Route to Scotland—as "Special Scotch Express". No one seems to know exactly when, or by whom, the trains acquired the nickname of "Flying Scotsman" and many years were to elapse before, in the days when the three railways just mentioned had become a part of the London & North Eastern Railway, the title "Flying Scotsman" was adopted officially.

No other British express can lay claim to so lengthy a record of an unchanged starting time. Certainly in the southbound direction between 1862 and 1876 the start from Edinburgh at different periods varied between 10.10, 10.15, 10.20 and 10.25 am, but in 1876 it came back to 10.00 and has so remained without a break until now. Going north, the only brief change from the 10.00 start out of Kings Cross was in 1917 and 1918, the last year of the First World War, when it became 9.30; with this brief exception, for 108 years on end, up to 1969, we have had the "Flying Scotsman" making its exit from London on the stroke of ten o'clock. What *has* radically changed, on the other hand, is the journey time; who in 1862 could have dreamed that the $10\frac{1}{2}$ hours of the first years would have shrunk by 1966 to 5 hours 50 minutes?

For some years after it first began to run, the "Flying Scotsman" followed, over three different sections of its journey, a course different from the

◀ The historic non-stop journey of May 1, 1968; No. 4472 climbs away from Kings Cross past the old connection to Top Shed, neck and neck with the Deltic-hauled regular 10 am "Flying Scotsman" to Edinburgh.

[Patrick Russell

East Coast main line of to-day. From what is now Shaftholme Junction, $4\frac{1}{2}$ miles north of Doncaster, there was no direct line in 1862 to York. The Great Northern engines used the tracks of the then Lancashire & Yorkshire Railway to Knottingley, after which a spur line of the North Eastern Railway took them through Ferrybridge to Burton Salmon, where they joined the latter's main line from Normanton to York. Not until 1871 did the North Eastern Railway open its direct line from Shaftholme to York by way of Selby, to which the "Flying Scotsman" was then transferred.

Further north, after the "Flying Scotsman" had passed Ferryhill, for its first ten years it had to follow the old NER route by way of Leamside and Penshaw to Gateshead, but in 1872 there came the transfer to the new Team Valley line, taking the train for the first time through Durham and over the viaduct which gave its passengers such a fine view of Durham Cathedral in its impressive location above the River Wear. The final change of route did not come about until 1906, when the great new King Edward VII bridge across the Tyne gorge cut out the circuit through Gateshead and over Stephenson's old High Level Bridge into Newcastle Central Station. Also for the first time this re-routing made it possible for the "Flying Scotsman" to run through Newcastle without the reversal in the Central Station which had been necessary up till then.

When it first began to run, the "Flying Scoisman", as already mentioned, took $10\frac{1}{2}$ hr. from London to reach Edinburgh. The first 4 hr. 25 min. was spent in reaching York, including various stops; one of these was Retford, where a through portion was detached for Sheffield and Manchester. This was long before the days of restaurant cars, and passengers were therefore allowed 30 min. at York in order that those who so wished might swallow a hasty lunch in the capacious dining room at that station; so the halt here lasted from 2.25 to 2.55 pm. Eventually it was 8.30 pm before the through passengers found themselves in the Waverley Station at Edinburgh. In the opposite direction the "Flying Scotsman" took no less than 11½ hr. to complete its journey. However, by the time that both the Shaftholme–Selby–York and the Team Valley lines had come into use in 1876 the overall times in both directions had diminished to 9 hr., a considerable improvement.

Matters then remained without much change until in November, 1887, the three East Coast partners decided that they would allow third-class passengers into the exclusive precincts of the "Flying Scotsman"; up till then, like the rival 10.00 am of the West Coast Route from Euston, this train had admitted first and second class travellers only. When the West Coast partners realised in 1888 that they were losing third-class passengers to the rival route, they decided that something drastic must be done. What they did do, keeping their intentions secret until the last minute, was to announce that from June 2 their "Day Scotch Express" the 10.00 am from Euston, would be accelerated by a full hour from Euston to Edinburgh, so for the first time equalling the East Coast 9 hr., and over a route longer by 7 miles.

This precipitated what has always since been known as the 1888 "Race to Edinburgh". On both sides of the country acceleration succeeded acceleration until by early August the schedules had come down to 8 hr., and from August 13 the East Coast authorities announced that the "Flying Scotsman" would run from Kings Cross to Edinburgh in 7¾ hr. Actually the fastest West Coast time made in this historic contest was 7 hr. 38 min., from Euston to Edinburgh Princes Street on August 7, but this the "Flying Scotsman" of the East Coast beat on August 31 with a time of 7 hr. 27 min., notwithstanding delay at Selby waiting at the swing-bridge for a hay barge to drift by on the River Aire, a tedious holding until the scheduled departure time by the North Eastern authorities at York, and a dead stand for signals at Ferryhill. After this, by common consent, the "Race" came to an end, and both sides agreed that the time of the "Flying Scotsman" should not be cut below 8¼ hr., and that the West Coast Route should be content with a minimum of 8½ hr.

Nothing more of note happened until 1895, when another "Race" came about; this was due to the opening of the Forth and Tay Bridges, which had allowed the East Coast partners greatly to reduce their schedules from London to Dundee and Aberdeen. This time the "Race" was over a much longer distance, to Aberdeen, and Edinburgh had

no immediate concern in it other than that on the fastest East Coast night, August 21, the eight o'clock night sleeper from Kings Cross put in an appearance at Edinburgh Waverley at 2.19 in the morning, after a run of no more than 6 hr. 19 min. from London and also after some most reckless speeding round curves.

When the 1895 "Race" was over, the East and West Coast Routes came to an agreement that with their night trains the minimum time between Kings Cross and Edinburgh and Euston and Glasgow should be 7¾ hr. and 8 hr. respectively, and that both the "Flying Scotsman" and the 10.00 am from Euston to Edinburgh Waverley should take not less than 8¼ hr.—a pact destined to remain in force for no less than 37 years, until May, 1932. By this time the Anglo-Scottish trains were falling in speed so far behind other main line services in Great Britain that the word "Flying" in the title of the East Coast "Scotsman" had become almost a joke.

Although the time allowed at York for lunch had been cut to 10 min. after the introduction of restaurant cars in 1900, the overall time of the train still remained 8¼ hr., with occasional point-to-point adjustments in the schedules. Over the Great Northern Railway 105.5 miles from Kings Cross to Grantham the down "Scotsman" was allowed two hours flat—52.7 mph average—while over the easier 82.7 miles to York, 97 min. was conceded, a fall in speed to 51.2 mph. No higher speeds were maintained over the North Eastern section despite the fact of being dead level for the major part of the distance; the 80.6 miles from York to Newcastle via Gateshead occupied 92 min., average 52.5 mph, and the 67.0 miles on to Berwick 77 min., at 52.2 mph. It was the North British Railway which had the easiest task with the "Scotsman", however, for 81 min. was allowed for the final 57.5 miles into Edinburgh, an average of no more than 42.6 mph. And notwithstanding this ultra-liberal concluding allowance, the timetables of the 1900's contained the threatening note, "Connections beyond Edinburgh are not guaranteed by this train." North Eastern locomotives worked the train through from Newcastle to Edinburgh.

Southbound, the "Flying Scotsman" up till the 1932 accelerations was pursuing an equally unhurried course. From Edinburgh to Berwick, including the 1 in 96 climb of Cockburnspath bank, the train was scheduled to run in 8 min. less than the ridiculous 81 min. going north; this allowance was 73 min. Then followed 78 min. from Berwick to Newcastle and 47 min. for the 36.6 (later 36.1) miles from Newcastle to Darlington, where the "Flying Scotsman" deigned to make a stop which it did not make in the down direction. Over the level racing ground from Darlington to York no less than 49 min. were conceded start to stop for the 44.1 miles—what an extraordinary contrast with the $30\frac{1}{2}$ min. pass-to-pass allowance of the same train to-day! Finally the Great Northern had 97 min. to work the train from York to Grantham and 122 min. on to Kings Cross. When at last in May, 1932, the abrogation of the 1895 agreement took place, acceleration had become urgent, and vastly more powerful locomotives were now available to make possible the drastic cuts in time that took place.

This brings us to a brief review of the way in which the motive power itself developed over the years on the East Coast Route. Consideration will be limited to the products of Doncaster Works of the Great Northern Railway, which eventually were to monopolise the working of the "Flying Scotsman" and other East Coast expresses over the entire route. From 1870 onwards no more than three different designs, each of which was to provide a sensation in the locomotive world by being a complete departure from previous practice, and each designed by a succession of three notable Locomotive Superintendents or Chief Mechanical Engineers, for the next three-quarters of a century were to work the "Flying Scotsman" out of Kings Cross and eventually through to Edinburgh.

The first of these was Patrick Stirling's famous 4-2-2 design, the first of which, appropriately GNR No. 1, emerged from Doncaster "Plant" in 1870. Of this engine the most notable feature was the 8ft. $1\frac{1}{2}$ in. diameter of the driving wheels, to give these single-drivers, which Stirling always favoured, a better grip on the rails, he explained. With these wheels he fitted cylinders of 18 in. diameter and the unusually long stroke of 28 in.; and although he would have preferred a 2-2-2 design, because he had no love for bogies, a 4-2-2 wheel arrangement was unavoidable, as otherwise he would have had too much overhang at the leading end. As with all his engines, Stirling did not provide any dome, and the long domeless barrel, with a tall chimney at one end, a brass safety-valve casing at the other, together with the graceful curved sides of the smokebox down to the cylinders and the great slotted splashers over the driving wheels, gave the Stirling "eight-footers" an appearance that was unique.

It was these handsome engines that worked the racing trains over the Great Northern section of the main line in the exciting weeks of 1888 and 1895. The climax of the latter was when No. 668 passed Peterborough, 76.4 miles from Kings Cross, in 72 min., averaged all but a mile-a-minute up the long bank to Stoke Summit, and reached Grantham, 105.5 miles, in 101 min.; while No. 775 continued the good work by covering the 82.7 miles from Grantham to York in 76 min.—a total running time of 3 min. under 3 hr., and this away back in 1895. But the load was no more than six of the light coaches of the period, mostly six-wheelers, weighing with passengers and luggage about 105 tons.

Stirling retired at the end of 1895, and his place at Doncaster was taken by H. A. Ivatt, under whom a drastic development in design was destined to take place. Dining cars were beginning to come into use, and to give access to the restaurants this meant corridor coaches, and more of them in order to provide the same seating space. In the last years of his reign Stirling mistakenly had tried to give his later "eight-footers" more tractive power by providing them with even bigger cylinders, $19\frac{1}{2}$ in. diameter by 28 in. stroke, but their unaltered small boilers were not big enough to provide such cylinders with an adequate supply of steam. Something drastic needed to be done, and Ivatt was the man to do it.

So it was that in 1898, 28 years after Stirling's first 4-2-2, there appeared from Doncaster Works Britain's first 4-4-2, Ivatt's No. 990. There could hardly have been a more complete reversal of a predecessor's policy than the proportions embodied in this engine. Instead of $19\frac{1}{2}$ in. by 28 in. cylinders there were now cylinders no bigger than $18\frac{3}{4}$ in. diameter by 24 in. stroke; instead of single driving wheels of 8 ft. $1\frac{1}{2}$ in. diameter, 6 ft. $7\frac{1}{2}$ in. coupled wheels; and instead of a boiler with no more than 1,032 sq. ft. heating surface and a firegrate area of 20 sq. ft., the new 4-4-2 had a heating surface of 1,442 sq. ft. and a firegrate area of 26.8 sq. ft. The odd result was that Ivatt's Atlantic had a nominal tractive effort of 15,850 lb., whereas that of Stirling's last 4-2-2s was 16,100 lb. But the tractive force formula means nothing unless there is sufficient steam to make it effective; Ivatt had publicly proclaimed it as his opinion that the capacity of a locomotive was its "ability to boil water", and here was the principle in action. There was no question, of course, as to which actually was the more powerful of the two types.

Now as previously mentioned train weights were rapidly increasing. Even to the end of the last century such a train as the "Flying Scotsman" still included six-wheel coaches in its formation, and still had its lengthy lunch stop at York. But in 1900 a revolutionary change took place. It was the introduction of two new trains, of American design and appearance, each composed of eight bow-ended 65 ft. 6in. long twelve-wheel cars, restaurant cars included, and weighing in all 265 tons. Similar new coaching stock on other Anglo-Scottish trains and on the London-Leeds service so increased train-loads generally that Ivatt took another step to improve the water-boiling ability of his engines, and it was sensational indeed. It was the introduction in 1902 of his first large-boiled Atlantic, No. 251, which with its 5 ft. 6 in. diameter boiler seemed a more monstrous machine than any which had been seen before on British metals.

Apart from the far larger boiler, the remainder of the engine was practically identical with the first Ivatt Atlantic, No. 990, for which reason I have regarded these two types jointly as the second development in the series of three designs to which I referred earlier. Now the disparity between the Ivatt 4-4-2 and the Stirling 4-2-2 was greater than ever; the heating surface of the big-boilered Atlantic, 2,500 sq. ft., was more than twice that of the Stirling "eight-footer", and the firegrate area, 31 sq. ft., more than half as much again as the 4-2-2's 20 sq. ft. The 31 sq. ft. had been made possible because in No. 251 Ivatt, with no coupled wheels under the cab, had used the space so made available to spread a wide fire box across the main frames of the engine, instead of dropping a deep firebox between them, as was the normal practice.

From 1903 onwards, as the large-boilered Atlantics began to multiply, the Great Northern Railway had a type which was to work the "Flying Scotsman" and other East Coast expresses between Kings Cross and York for the next twenty years. Before their termination, however, Ivatt had been succeeded in 1911 at Doncaster by the most famous Chief Mechanical Engineer that that locomotive works has ever known, H. N. Gresley, or, as he was later to be known, Sir Nigel Gresley. Once again a crisis was impending in the working of the East Coast expresses, which were growing steadily in weight. By now the Ivatt Atlantics had all been superheated,

◀ A typical East Coast route express at about the turn of the century, headed by Stirling 8 ft 4-2-2 No. 663.
[Locomotive Publishing Co

▶ By 1914 East Coast expresses were largely in the hands of the Ivatt Atlantics; large boilered 4-4-2 No. 1451 heads through Oakleigh Park with a train of 12-wheelers, most of which are clerestory cars of about 1900.   [Locomotive Publishing Co

▼ The pioneer Gresley GNR Pacific No. 1470 *Great Northern*.

many with 32-element superheaters, and had had their cylinders enlarged to 20 in. diameter. Once they had got on the move they were capable of handling quite heavy trains at speed; of this I had proof for myself on a memorable occasion when No. 4404, taking over at Grantham the 17-coach 585-ton "Heart of Midlothian" from a Gresley Pacific which had run hot, covered the 82.7 miles to York in 87 min. 40 sec. or 86½ min. net, with speed even on level track up to 75 mph. But the limited adhesion of 36 tons with two coupled axles only made the Atlantics slow in starting and running uphill; something considerably more powerful was needed for reliable performance with the heavier trains.

This reliability Gresley had set out to provide when in 1922 there emerged from Doncaster Works his first Pacific—No. 1470 *Great Northern*. Whereas from 300 to 400 tare tons had normally been regarded as the maximum in ordinary working for the Ivatt 4-4-2s, Gresley announced confidently that his new 4-6-2 would be capable of handling 600-ton trains on the existing schedules. To say that *Great Northern* provided a sensation in the

locomotive world would be to put it mildly; I still have vivid recollections of the impression made on my own mind when I first saw the engine on exhibition at Kings Cross terminus. Britain had seen one Pacific before, *The Great Bear* of the Great Western Railway, completed in 1908, far from successful in performance, and nothing like as impressive in appearance as GNR No. 1470, shortly afterwards joined by No. 1471. Gresley lost no time in proving his contention by working No. 1471 on a special 20-coach 617-ton train from Kings Cross to Grantham on the 120 min. schedule of the "Flying Scotsman", which it observed without difficulty.

Once again a revolutionary development had taken place in Great Northern Railway motive power. The sequence of that development had been quite a logical one—from 4-2-2 to 4-4-2, and from 4-4-2 to 4-6-2. One of the principal gains had been in adhesion weight, from Stirling's 19.7 tons to Ivatt's 36.0 tons and now to Gresley's 60.0 tons. Boiler heating surfaces, at first without and later with superheaters, had progressed from 1,032 sq. ft. to 2,500 sq. ft. and now to 2,930 sq. ft., and firegrate areas from 20.0 past 31.0 to 41.25 sq. ft. Working steam pressures had not greatly changed; although the first of Stirling's 4-2-2s had carried a pressure of 140 lb./sq. in. only, his final design worked at 170 lb., and this was not greatly exceeded by Gresley's 180 lb. But in the process of development the nominal tractive effort of the engines had been almost doubled, and Gresley's big boiler, 5 ft. 6 in. diameter at the front end and tapering out to 6 ft. 5 in. diameter at the rear end, with its capacious firebox spread out over the frames, was certainly not going to fall short of generating sufficient steam to make the tractive effort effective.

Nos. 1470 and 1471 had barely got into their stride before, at the beginning of 1923, the Great Northern Railway lost its identity in the much larger London & North Eastern group, but fortunately with Gresley still in command at Doncaster as LNER Chief Mechanical Engineer. The performance of the two new giants had proved so successful that mass production of the class was a foregone conclusion, and from 1923 to 1925 no fewer than fifty of these engines were built. The first of them to emerge from "Plant" in January, 1923, was destined to become the most famous of all the Class A1 Pacifics, and to be seen over more main lines in the country than any other British locomotive. It is actually the subject of this book—No. 1472 *Flying Scotsman*, soon after its

▲ No. 4472 in the condition in which it was exhibited at the Wembley Exhibition in 1924. [W. J. Reynolds

◄ No. 4472 as built. This engine was under construction in the last months of 1922 and was delivered in January 1923, a week or two after the Great Northern Railway had become part of the LNER. The engine thus appeared with its planned GNR number 1472, but with the letters "L&NER" on the tender.

► To give the locomotives wider route availability the LNER Pacifics, including No. 4472, were given lower domes, chimneys and cab roofs. Some were also given new high-sided tenders, a few of which were fitted with corridors. This is the condition in which No. 4472 appeared for its non-stop run in 1928.

construction, in the general LNER renumbering scheme, to carry the number 4472.

In the year 1924 there was held at Wembley what was called the British Empire Exhibition, and it was planned that *Flying Scotsman* in person should represent the LNER on their stand. With a view also to its use subsequently on Royal trains when required, it was decided to embellish No. 4472 in various ways not shared by the other Pacifics. These included brass rims to the coupled wheel splashers, burnished tyres, and the new LNER coat-of-arms on the cab sides. Incidentally, soon after the exhibition the chimney, dome and cab roof of No. 4472 and the other early Pacifics had

been cut down to enable them to pass the more restricted North British loading gauge, and so to run through to Edinburgh.

The exhibition of *Flying Scotsman* at Wembley had an unforeseen result. On an adjacent stand the Great Western Railway was exhibiting its new 4-6-0, No. 4073 *Caerphilly Castle*, and each of the proud owners was claiming for its exhibit the distinction of being the most powerful express locomotive type in the country. Not surprisingly here was a dispute which could only be resolved by a comparative test in identical running conditions. This was arranged in the following year, 1925, when a Gresley Pacific worked for a fortnight over the GWR main line between Paddington and Plymouth in competition with a GWR Castle, and a Castle tried its strength against a Gresley 4-6-2 between Kings Cross and Doncaster.

Surprisingly, however, neither *Flying Scotsman* nor *Caerphilly Castle* were the engines selected; it was LNER No. 4474 *Victor Wild* that worked down to Plymouth, and GWR No. 4079 *Pendennis Castle* that showed its paces between Kings Cross and Doncaster. Another event in which perhaps *Flying Scotsman* might have been expected to participate was the great Centenary Procession of 1925, over the route of the old Stockton & Darlington Railway, but actually the two LNER Pacifics chosen to participate were Gresley's No. 2563 *William Whitelaw*, and, from the former North Eastern Railway, Raven's No. 2400 *City of Newcastle*, the latter heading the train of new "Flying Scotsman" stock.

It was three years later, in 1928, when *Flying Scotsman* next came into the limelight. With the formation of the London & North Eastern and London Midland & Scottish Railways, each of the two competing routes from London to Scotland had come under the control of a single company throughout its length, and competition between them still continued, now with considerably greater resources than before to make it effective. The hampering post-1895 agreement still made it impossible to compete in the matter of time, so other prestige attractions had to be devised. One was more comfortable rolling stock; a second was in the length of run which could be timetabled without intermediate stop. The latter had to be confined to the summer, when there would be sufficient through passengers to fill a non-stop train.

So it was that in July, 1927, the LMSR, having provided its 10.00 am from Euston and the corresponding 10.00 am from Glasgow and Edinburgh with a brand new 15-coach train, and named it the "Royal Scot", advertised the train as non-stop over the whole course, though actually stopping at Carnforth, 236.2 miles from Euston, to change engines, and at Symington to divide or unite the Glasgow and Edinburgh portions. The LNER promptly replied by booking the "Flying Scotsman" to run non-stop over the 268.3 miles between Kings Cross and Newcastle, with the relief train which always ran during the summer months making the "Scotsman's" other regular stops. But in September of the same year the LMSR, now in possession of its new Royal Scot 4-6-0 locomotives, presented the LNER with a much bigger prestige problem by beginning a regular non-stop run of 301.1 miles between Euston and Kingmoor, Carlisle. This the LMSR continued to do through that winter; but by the spring of 1928, however, the LNER already had a plan which the LMSR could not beat as a daily proposition.

This was to create a world record by running the "Flying Scotsman" non-stop over the entire 392.7 miles in each direction between Kings Cross and Edinburgh. As it was realised that a continuous working of over 8 hr. would be too much to expect of a single crew, means had to be devised of changing the crew at the half-way point without stopping the train. Gresley therefore designed and built in great secrecy at Doncaster some tenders with corridor passages through them, which could be vestibuled to the leading coach of the train in which a compartment would be reserved for the second crew. Doncaster also had produced for the occasion a new "Flying Scotsman" train, with such

additional amenities as a hairdressing compartment and a ladies' retiring room, which would have a lady attendant. The inaugural day was to be May 1.

But the LMSR had decided that the LNER should not have all the limelight, and with mischievous humour three days earlier, and also after secret preparation, divided its down "Royal Scot" and ran both portions through without any intermediate stop; the Glasgow portion thus made a non-stop run of 401.4 miles and the Edinburgh portion one of 399.7 miles, both longer than the LNER 392.7 miles. But this was no more than a flash in the pan, and would have been out of the question as a daily performance. Moreover, the attention that it attracted in the daily press was no more than a fraction of what the LNER obtained on the inauguration of its daily London-Edinburgh non-stop journey on the following Monday.

For the first down run the engine was none other than No. 4472 *Flying Scotsman*, at the head of a 386-ton train. The driver was A. Pibworth, who also drove No. 4475 *Flying Fox* on the "Flying Scotsman's" first Kings Cross-Newcastle non-stop run of the previous year. This time he only drove as far as Alne, where North Eastern Area driver T. Blades took over. One rather absurd feature of the new schedule was that because of the time agreement with the LMSR, the "Flying Scotsman", with all intermediate stops cut out, could not be publicly booked into Edinburgh before 6.15 pm. On the first down run it arrived at 6.03 pm after the easiest of running, with some 2 tons of coal still left unused on the tender.

One of the lessons which Gresley had had to learn from the locomotive exchange with the Great Western Railway Castle 4-6-0s in 1925 was that the performance of his Pacific could be greatly improved if their piston-valves were given a longer travel and a longer lap, so that they could be worked at speed, like the GWR engines, with fully open regulators and in short cut-offs; in this way their average coal consumption had been brought down from 50 to 38 lb. per mile. Among the other Class A1 Pacifics No. 4472 *Flying Scotsman* had had its valve-motion so adjusted, which explains why the 392.7 mile run was completed successfully on an average coal consumption of no more than 39 lb. to the mile.

Six years were now to elapse before *Flying Scotsman* was again to earn encomia and this time it was to be by a performance which would break a whole sheaf of records. The year was 1934, and spurred on by the success of the German high speed "Flying Hamburger" the LNER management had decided, in celebration in 1935 of the 25 years' reign of King George V, to introduce a similar service between Kings Cross and Newcastle, in 4 hr. for the 268.3 miles, but worked by steam power. Some preliminary trials needed to be made, and accordingly it was decided that a special train should be run from Kings Cross, first of all not to Newcastle but to Leeds and back. The date decided on was November 30, 1934, and the locomotive picked for the trip was *Flying Scotsman*.

By now the engine was being manned regularly by Driver W. Sparshatt, and he and his fireman, R. Webster, made an ideal combination for the task in hand. A train of four coaches had been assembled, including the dynamometer car, and weighing with the small party on board 147 tons. The schedule laid down for the 185.7 miles was 165 min.

The special started from No. 11 platform at Kings Cross, in what was called the Local station, with some sharply curved track leading into Gasworks Tunnel. Sparshatt opened up with such vigour that the speed over these connections was considerably above normal, and some suspicious markings afterwards were found on some of the check rails, but fortunately nothing untoward resulted. Then began a performance which shattered every record that had been made down the Great Northern main line to that date.

It included such times as 32 min. 17 sec. for the 44.5 miles from Hitchin to Peterborough, passed in 60 min, 39 sec; an average of 82.5 mph up the whole of the 10-mile climb to Stoke Summit; a time of two hours precisely for the first 153¾ miles from London; Doncaster passed in an unprecedented 122 min. 27 sec. from the terminus; and Leeds Central reached in 151 min. 56 sec. So far as published records go, though modern Deltic diesels have worked trains down to Leeds in 2½ hr. net or slightly over, *Flying Scotsman's* actual time of just under 152 min. has not yet been beaten. So the 165 min. schedule had been improved on by 13 min.

In view of this gain, the authorities decided that the return journey should be made with a heavier load; two coaches were therefore added, bringing

the weight up to 207 tons. Again the performance was brilliant in the extreme, and the climax was when, in the descent from Stoke Summit, *Flying Scotsman* reached Britain's first 100 mph fully authenticated by the unerring record of the dynamometer car. A top speed of 102½ mph had certainly been claimed in 1904 for the Great Western Railway 4-4-0 *City of Truro*, but subsequent research into the contradictory figures left by the recorder on that occasion have made it pretty clear that the actual maximum cannot have exceeded 96 or 97 mph. The distinction of having achieved the first three-figure speed on British rails therefore rests fairly and squarely with *Flying Scotsman*.

This was not all, however. Coming up, 8 min. had been gained on the test schedule by Peterborough, but Fireman Webster was now tiring. This was small wonder after his strenuous labours on this 372-mile high speed round, so no more time was gained to Kings Cross. Even so, the terminus was reached in 157 min. 17 sec., 7¾ min. inside the scheduled 2¾ hr., and in 5¾ min. less than the fastest booked time to-day with a 3,300 hp Deltic diesel. In the one day, *Flying Scotsman* had averaged 90 mph for 40 miles, and 80 mph for 250 miles; 371.6 miles, including two starts and two stops, and a number of severe service slacks, had been covered at a mean speed of 72.1 mph.

◄ No. **4472** *Flying Scotsman* heads the train of that name past Greenwood box in the mid-1930s.

[E. R. Wethersett

▲ No. **4472** also appeared in films; here it is seen alongside a special train carrying a camera crew used for train-to-train action shots.

Fireman Webster had performed the herculean task of shifting some 9 tons of coal in a single working day, which works out at an average of 54 lb. per mile—certainly heavy, but *Flying Scotsman* also was being given little respite, with cut-off advanced to as much as 40 per cent on the harder uphill stretches. Yet the engine was perfectly cool in every bearing at the end of each run. Most remarkable of all, perhaps, was that up to the date of this run *Flying Scotsman* had covered a total of over 653,000 miles in eleven years in heavy express work, and 44,176 miles since its last heavy repair—a tribute indeed to the excellence of Doncaster building and Kings Cross maintenance.

Reference has been made previously to the lessons learned by Gresley from the exchange trial with the Great Western Railway in 1925—how to improve his valve-setting. Another lesson was the usefulness of the GWR working steam pressure of 225 lb./sq. in; this in conjunction with Churchward's long-travel long-lap valve-setting made it possible for GWR engines to be worked in short cut-offs, which in its turn increased overall thermal efficiency by making better use of the expansive properties of the steam. Gresley had learned this lesson also when in 1927 he rebuilt A1 Pacifics Nos. 2544 *Lemberg* and 4480 *Enterprise* with new boilers carrying a working pressure of 220 lb./sq. in. The results were so successful that eventually the whole of the original A1 Pacifics were rebuilt in the same way, No. 4472 *Flying Scotsman* among their number. One associated change, which did not improve the appearance of *Flying Scotsman*, was the substitution for the original dome of the unsightly so-called

"banjo dome" which eventually became the standard for all the Gresley Pacifics.

To complete the story, though strictly this has nothing to do with *Flying Scotsman*, mention must be made of the final Gresley Pacific design, the streamlined A4, the first examples of which took the rails in 1935 for the working of the new 4 hr. "Silver Jubilee" express between Kings Cross and Newcastle. As is seen in the table of leading dimensions on page 21 of all the classes from the Stirling 4-2-2s and Ivatt 4-4-2s to the various developments of the Gresley Pacifics, the principal change from the A3 dimensions was that the A4s had their working pressure lifted from 220 to 250 lb./sq. in., which despite a reduction in cylinder diameter to 18½ in. boosted the tractive effort from 32,910 to 35,455 lb.

But the developments in the A4s that really mattered were the complete streamlining of the steam passages as well as the external streamlining and, of course, the valve-setting. Following the triumph of *Flying Scotsman* in being the first British locomotive to reach 100 mph, these changes enabled A4 No. 2509 *Silver Link* to be the only

◀ No. 4472 in the condition in which it ran in the early part of 1948 carrying its 1946 number, 103, with the legend "British Railways" on the tender. It was photographed here running-in on a local train near Wakefield after overhaul at Doncaster.
[Leslie Overend

▼ *Flying Scotsman* was later renumbered as BR No. 60103 and rebuilt with a double chimney. In this condition it is seen working the down "Yorkshire Pullman" near Hadley Wood in 1960. [Derek Cross

British steam locomotive ever to have covered 40 miles on end at an average of 100 mph, and No. 4468 *Mallard* to create a world record for steam with a maximum speed of 126 mph.

After Gresley's untimely death in 1941, Edward Thompson, who succeeded him as Chief Mechanical Engineer, began a more systematic renumbering of LNER locomotives, in the course of which *Flying Scotsman* at first became No. 502 and later No. 103. Then, in 1946, there came the succession of A. H. Peppercorn to the position of control at Doncaster, and the emergence of another express passenger Pacific design; this he classified as a new A1 series, the remaining Pacifics of the original A1 series which as yet had not been rebuilt with 220 lb. boilers being reclassified as A10. But it did not take many years for the A10 class to disappear. The final change for *Flying Scotsman* was in the renumbering of the whole of the locomotive stock of British Railways which followed nationalisation in 1948, in which this engine became No. 60103. But after the purchase of this locomotive by A. F. Pegler in 1963 the number 4472 was restored, though the final Class A3 developments, including the banjo dome, remained.

By 1949, with 34 of the A4 and 50 of the new A1 Pacifics in service, the A3 Pacifics for the most part had been relegated to secondary duties, and the zenith of *Flying Scotsman's* achievements by now was past. Then began the infiltration of diesel power, and with the appearance in 1961 of the first of the 3,300 hp Deltic diesels and in 1962 of the 2,750 hp Brush diesels which eventually were to be multiplied to a total of 510 units, the writing was on the wall for the whole of the Pacifics. To-day steam traction in Great Britain has come to an end, and we have reached the stage when Deltic diesels have cut the daily time of the "Flying Scotsman" to 5 hr. 50 min. between Kings Cross and Edinburgh, while raising maximum speeds to long stretches at 100 mph.

But we have reason to be grateful to Mr. Pegler for the preservation of *Flying Scotsman*, not merely as a museum piece, but for some years of active life in hauling special trains all over the country for nostalgic locomotive lovers. Few could have imagined it possible that the locomotive which worked the first world record non-stop "Flying Scotsman" from King Cross to Edinburgh on May 1, 1928, would repeat this feat forty years later, on May 1, 1968, at the ripe age of 45 years.

▼ During 1949 *Flying Scotsman* was still running in LNER green livery but carrying its new number, 60103, with "British Railways" in full on the tender. It was photographed with the 10.15 am Leeds–Kings Cross train near Potters Bar on April 9, 1949.

[E. D. Bruton

▶ *Flying Scotsman* in its final BR guise on August 8, 1962, with wing type smoke deflectors.   M. Dunnett

DEVELOPMENT OF GREAT NORTHERN AND LONDON & NORTH EASTERN LOCOMOTIVE POWER

Designer	Stirling	Ivatt		Gresley		
Type Wheel arrangement	As built ‡ 4-2-2	As built 4-4-2	Superheated 4-4-2	Class A1 4-6-2	Class A3 4-6-2	Class A4 4-6-2
Cylinder, diameter	(2) 19½ in.	(2) 18¾ in.	(2) 20 in.	(3) 20 in.	(3) 19 in.	(3) 18½ in.
,, stroke	28 in.	24 in.	24 in.	26 in.	26 in.	26 in.
Driving wheels, diameter	8 ft. 1½ in.	6 ft. 7½ in.	6 ft. 7½ in.	6 ft. 8 in.	6 ft. 8 in.	6 ft. 8 in.
Heating surface:—						
tubes (and flues)	910 sq. ft.	2,359 sq. ft.	1,824 sq. ft.	2,715 sq. ft.	2,477 sq. ft.	2.345 sq. ft.
firebox	122 sq. ft.	141 sq. ft.	141 sq. ft.	215 sq. ft.	215 sq. ft.	231 sq. ft.
total evaporative	1,032 sq. ft.	2,500 sq. ft.	1,965 sq. ft.	2,930 sq. ft.	2,692 sq. ft.	2,576 sq. ft.
Superheating surface	—	—	‖568 sq. ft.	525 sq. ft.	706 sq. ft.	750 sq. ft.
Firegrate area	20.0 sq. ft.	31.0 sq. ft.	31.0 sq. ft.	41.25 sq. ft.	41.25 sq. ft.	41.25 sq. ft.
Working pressure	170 lb./sq. in.	175 lb./sq. in.	170 lb./sq. in.	180 lb./sq. in.	220 lb./sq. in.	250 lb./sq. in.
Tractive effort*	16,100 lb.	15,850 lb.	17,450 lb.	29,835 lb.	32,910 lb.	35,455 lb.
Adhesion weight	19.7 tons	36.0 tons	36.0 tons	60.0 tons	66.15 tons	66.0 tons
Engine weight†	49.5 tons	68.3 tons	69.4 tons	92.45 tons	96.25 tons	102.95 tons
Tender capacity, coal	5 tons	6½ tons	6½ tons	9 tons	9 tons	9 tons
,, ,, water	3,850 gal.	3,500 gal.	3,500 gal.	5,000 gal.	5,000 gal.	5,000 gal.
,, weight, full	41.7 tons	43.1 tons	43.1 tons	¶56.3 tons	¶56.3 tons	§62.4 tons
Engine and tender weight	91.2 tons	111.4 tons	112.5 tons	¶148.75 tons	¶152.55 tons	§165.35 tons

* At 85 per cent working pressure † In working order ‡ Final series, built 1894
§ Corridor tender ¶ Add 6.1 tons if with corridor tender ‖ 32-element superheater

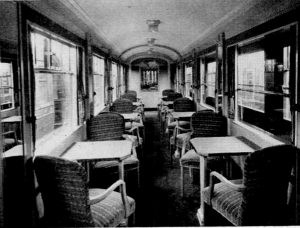

FLYING SCOTSMAN COACHES

▲ In LNER days the "Flying Scotsman" service was always provided with the latest type of rolling stock; this is the standard side-corridor composite of the early 1930s.　　　　　　　　[British Railways

◀ The buffet car of the 1948 "Flying Scotsman" set.

◀ The buffet with independent side corridor of the 1938 "Flying Scotsman" train.

▶ In contrast, the restaurant car of an East Coast Joint Stock first class diner of pre-1914 vintage.

Next page: No. 4472 in private ownership; *Flying Scotsman* leaves Hadley Wood North Tunnel with the empty stock of an excursion from Potters Bar to York on October 7, 1968.　　　　　　　　[V. C. K. Allen

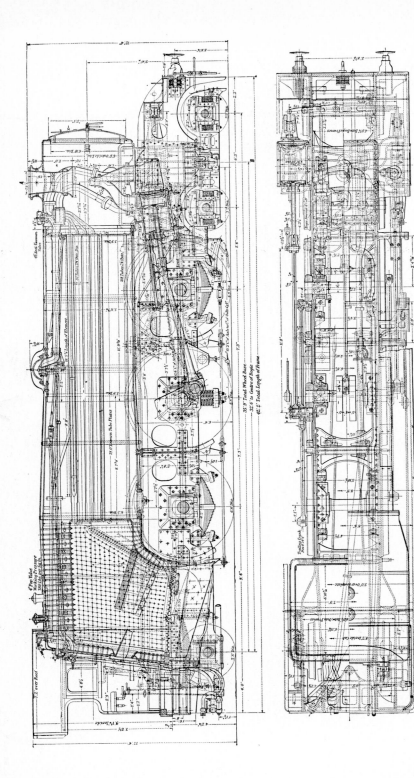

This plate is reprinted from "ENGINEERING"

General arrangement drawing of side and plan views of the first GN Pacific No. 1470, with which *Flying Scotsman* was similar. The end views of the locomotive are shown below.

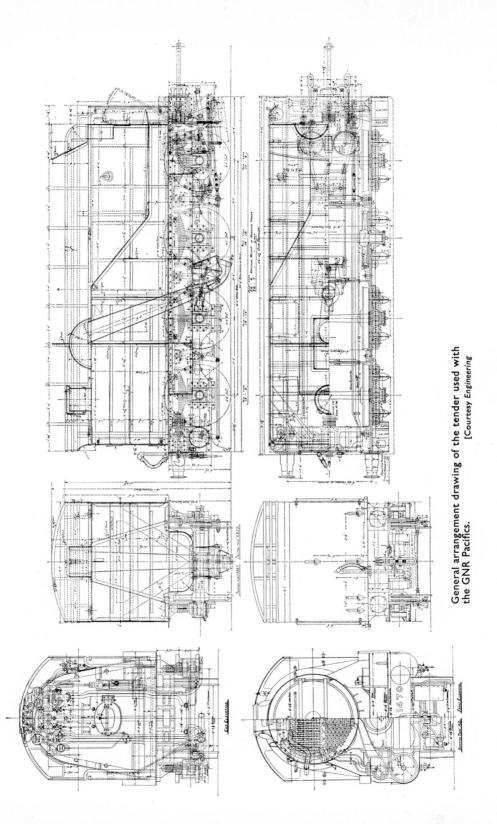

General arrangement drawing of the tender used with
the GNR Pacifics.
[Courtesy *Engineering*]

Living with No 4472

ALAN PEGLER

1954 WAS quite a year for me. After more than two years of negotiations I had control of the Festiniog Railway Company and not long afterwards I had a strange meeting in the buffet car of the old 7.25 am from Grantham to Kings Cross. The result of that meeting was a personal interview with Sir Brian Robertson, who asked me if I would join one of the Area Boards of the British Transport Commission, which were being set up at that time, as a part-time member. I accepted, and in February 1955 the Eastern Area Board held its first meeting at Liverpool Street. Over the next nine years I was to attend nearly a hundred of these meetings. It is probably true to say that if this had never happened 4472 *Flying Scotsman* would not be running today.

The railway bug bit me at a very tender age. It's always difficult to say with assurance what one's earliest recollections are, but I am pretty certain I can remember being taken in my pram to the level crossing at Barnby Moor & Sutton station (some 3½ miles north of Retford on the Great Northern main line). There I used to watch Ivatt Atlantics tearing along and there I saw my first Gresley Pacifics when I grew a little older. I was sent off to a prep school on the south coast and this of course meant a train journey (via London) of some 200 miles. Retford, my home station, was served by the celebrated 7.50 am from Leeds, which for many years ran non-stop from Retford to Kings Cross, and in the early 1930s claimed to be Europe's fastest train over a distance of more than 100 miles.

In 1928 I left Retford on May 8 on the first journey to my new school, but although I was only just eight years old I had been very thrilled by some events of the previous week. The "Flying Scotsman" train's non-stop services had been inaugurated on May 1 and as an already dedicated LNER fan, I

was greatly excited. I heard something about an LMS train making a run (two, in fact) of even greater length than the Kings Cross-Edinburgh direct route a day or two before, but I was old enough to gather that this was not the same thing at all as regular non-stop running right through the summer. I also gathered the engine had the same name as the train and this confused me terribly. How, I wondered, could this engine with the magical name *Flying Scotsman* be hauling a train non-stop from London to Edinburgh and a train from Edinburgh to London, simultaneously?

The answer was, of course, that it couldn't and didn't. There were already a number of Pacifics of Gresley's design running on the East Coast main line and another of the stud worked the other train in the opposite direction. 4472 *Flying Scotsman* was the elite, the special one of the class. Her embellishments testified to this—brass beading round the splashers of the driving wheels and a shiny external brilliance that seemed to excel all the others even in those clean-engine days. As if all this wasn't enough, my parents then revealed that it was this very engine whose cab I had stood in when she had been at the Empire Exhibition at Wembley a few years before.

Looking back I sometimes wonder whether this was what first forcibly brought home to me the difference between a cold steam locomotive and a hot one; a dead one and a live one. There seemed to be no connection between the showpiece inside an exhibition hall and the beautiful piece of machinery with its huge, striding wheels, flashing side rods and plumes of smoke and steam at the head of the train. That first non-stop "Flying Scotsman" run got a great deal of publicity, and every photograph that was published seemed to show the same engine, as if there were no other—No. 4472.

I was fourteen when 4472 hit the headlines again on test runs to Leeds (see page 17). Only five years later we were at war, high-speed train running was over, and *Flying Scotsman* became just

◀ No. 4472 at York in 1966. Although two tenders are available occasionally the locomotive can manage with only one tender on shorter runs.   [P. Hocquard

another locomotive, allocated to whatever duties might be required from day to day. Nationalisation after the war seemed to me, at the time, to be the ultimate disaster as even magic numbers like 4472 disappeared. After various changes, *Flying Scotsman* finally became Nationalised British Railways No. 60103; and that was the locomotive I kept my eye on when I found myself an Eastern Region Board member.

1962 saw the centenary of the 10 o'clock service from London to Edinburgh. No great ceremony took place, but a party of journalists did travel from Kings Cross on the "Flying Scotsman" train service. It so happened—I think more or less by chance—that 60103 was at Kings Cross on the morning of the departure of the Deltic diesel-hauled centenary train and someone had the idea of letting the steam locomotive remain in the adjoining platform while the Deltic pulled out. This was very swiftly sat on, however, and 60103 was sent off into the darkness of Gas Works Tunnel to be kept out of sight until after the Deltic had left.

I witnessed all this and felt very sorry for 60103. A few days later I started finding out how long it might be before she was withdrawn from service, and discovered that the vital date was likely to be early in 1963. A fund had been started in Edinburgh to save the locomotive, but when it became clear that not enough money was going to be raised I decided to step in and buy her myself. So it was that 60103 was sold to me straight out of traffic by the Eastern Region, not by the British Railways Central supplies organisation that has handled all other sales of locomotives since that date.

January 14, 1963 was a great day. It was also a very, very cold one. This was the winter of the great freeze-up and it is remarkable now to look at photographs of the deep snow that covered the country at that time. I travelled up to Kings Cross from Retford on the "Master Cutler" Pullman that morning, arriving in London soon after 10 o'clock. Transport had been laid on to take me out to "Top Shed" and there I found a battery of newsreel and TV cameras, and Fleet Street reporters. I spent two of the coldest hours I can ever remember being photographed inside 60103, in front of 60103 and in the cab of 60103, apart from making a number of recordings, some sound only and some in front of the camera.

Eventually it was time for *Flying Scotsman* to back on to her train, the 1.15 pm Leeds, in Kings Cross station. A really huge crowd had turned up to see us off and we got away to a great cheer, dead on time. The run was a good one and we got to Doncaster six minutes early. The normal diagram at that time was for the one locomotive to work straight through to Leeds, but on this occasion engines were changed at Doncaster and *Flying Scotsman* went straight into the "Plant", as Doncaster locomotive works has been known over the decades.

▶ A look inside *Flying Scotsman*; the boiler with tubes removed during the 1969 overhaul at Hunslet Works.

▼ *Flying Scotsman*'s boiler stripped ready for overhaul at Hunslet Works.

During the following weeks, various jobs were done that made a lot of difference to the locomotive's appearance. First and foremost the smoke deflectors were removed. These had been considered necessary because of the fitting of a double chimney not long before, but I also arranged for the double chimney and blastpipe to be replaced and a single chimney fitted again. This was not because I didn't believe in double chimneys—I was a staunch advocate of the conversion of the A3s from single chimneys and blastpipes to double—but double chimneys never *looked* right to me. I was very anxious for 4472 to look like a typical LNER A3 of the 1930s. It was really out of the question to consider trying to convert the loco-

motive to her original condition and I was prepared to settle for "typical A3" as a reasonable compromise.

A couple of trial trips with 12 coaches of empty stock were made between Doncaster and New England and then came the job of repainting in LNER livery. I little realised how soon that beautiful shiny paintwork would become dirty and cracked; over the next six years there were to be three more complete repaints and several major touchings-up involving the expenditure of items of money up to between £800 and £900 a time.

Running 4472 in 1963 was a comparatively straightforward business. There was plenty of steam about and few problems—none, really—

about finding suitable facilities for coaling and watering. Most routes were available, too, and places like Southampton and Exeter were visited during the first year of private ownership.

Four or five years later, however, it was a very different story and the national press, on November 28, 1967, carried stories of a British Railways Board official announcement of the previous day which said quite clearly that steam-hauled "specials" were to finish. No privately-preserved main line steam locomotives were permitted to run after the end of that year and even *Flying Scotsman's* future looked very uncertain. All the same, I had managed to get, in 1963, something that no other private owner succeeded in getting, namely Heads of Agreement between myself and BRB about arrangements for running 4472 up to mid-April, 1966. I had also succeeded in getting that date extended until April, 1971, so naturally I got to work at once endeavouring to have my own position clarified. The *Yorkshire Post*, on November 17, 1967 went so far as to print an article in which it was stated that *Flying Scotsman* was not subject to the ban on steam; although this subsequently turned out to be correct the story at that time was inspired guesswork. Many more months of delicate negotiations had to go on before the British Railways Board made it clear that they would honour the agreement in full; they then went one better and extended the time to December 31, 1971 instead of April 16.

Suddenly, therefore, it appeared as though 4472 was going to be the only privately-preserved main-line steam locomotive anyone was going to be able to see or travel behind during the next four years. In fact, when British Railways had themselves run their own last main-line steam tour on August 11, 1968 it became a fact that 4472 was the one and only in Britain.

This was a solemn thought, and also a great challenge. Needless to say, British Railways were not likely to look twice at any steam installation that was due for scrapping just for the sake of keeping one private owner happy, so early in 1968 plans had already been laid for making *Flying Scotsman* a completely self-contained unit, so far as this was practicable. A band of volunteer organisers, under George Hinchcliffe, was given the name of Flying Scotsman Enterprises, and under that comprehensive title everything to do with the running and maintenance of the locomotive is looked after. Various contractors are co-opted into the organisation, the main two being Bradshaws of Sturton-by-Stow, Lincolnshire who run the road coal lorry and water vehicles used for replenishing 4472 en route on any run, and Lloyd Davis, the coal factors in London, who regularly look after coaling in the London area.

On the British Railways side of the house, a special liaison officer was appointed to deal with me personally over the initiation of enquiries about any proposed runs. There are no short cuts in this system; he and I have to make contact with one another to approve every move of 4472, in broad principle, before anything can be started on in detail by other BR departments. This may sound cumbersome and slow, but in fact it is the opposite. The system really works remarkably well and since it came into being 4472 has succeeded in penetrating all sorts of places that would once have seemed most unlikely. Such things as doing a run from Liverpool Lime Street (under the electric traction wires) eleven weeks after the official "end of steam"—running direct from Hull to Bridlington and Scarborough, on the Great Eastern line between Ipswich and Norwich, and between Penistone and Huddersfield, to name just a few improbable concessions, chief of which was probably authority to negotiate the almost disused line between Melton Mowbray and Nottingham in September, 1968.

As most people know, a second corridor tender was fitted to 4472 in 1966. This gives a total water capacity of about 11,000 gallons, that can be replenished almost anywhere on any route by the road tanker, which holds 4,000 gallons. We can thus plan runs of between 200 and 250 miles (depending on the load) over routes completely devoid of any watering facilities whatsoever. Similarly, the coal lorry can, with the aid of the petrol driven conveyor, load about a ton of coal into the tender every five minutes, so refuelling is not a big problem. Sites must be chosen very carefully and here the close liaison with British Railways is indispensable. Without it the question of picking the right spot from BR's point of view and that of Flying Scotsman Enterprises could well take weeks.

▲ William Downie, railway mechanic specialist of the Canadian Transport Commission, Alan Pegler and George W. Johnston, chief boiler inspector of CNR, examine *Flying Scotsman* during its 1969 overhaul.

▶ *Flying Scotsman* in the process of being stripped at Hunslet Works.

▲ While the boiler was removed for overhaul in another part of Hunslet's workshops, other components were removed until all that was left was frames and wheels.

Bradshaws, of Sturton-by-Stow, a tiny and remote Lincolnshire village (also the home of George Hinchcliffe) man and run the road vehicles. They collect the selected Yorkshire coal from the NCB pithead at Rossington (just south of Doncaster), and 4472 is coaled with the aid of the conveyor at "Carr Loco", as the locomotive depot there has been known for many years.

When Carr Loco was a steam shed there were, of course, few problems, but now that it is a modern diesel depot special arrangements have to be made there for coaling, like everywhere else. When the depot was rebuilt it was possible to arrange for one "road" to be kept as a steam one, with a pit, watering facilities, and provision for washing out the boiler (needless to say, none of this could ever have happened without the agreement, which has been worth its weight in gold). Having coaled 4472, the road lorry almost invariably returns to Rossington pit to fill up again with coal and get ready to go, complete with the conveyor, to whatever appropriate refuelling point has been selected by the Flying Scotsman Enterprises and British Railways people concerned.

Water is usually obtainable from a hydrant at almost any point in Britain, so the road tanker seldom sets off from Lincolnshire with a full load. The usual drill is for the tanker to get away several hours in advance of the time it will be needed on a refuelling job, carrying perhaps a quarter or half its capacity load, and then, at a point nearest to where the rendezvous with 4472 is to be made, to fill up to capacity. Naturally, the water one gets in this way is hardly ever treated water, so water softening is arranged through the good offices of ICI, who made recommendations some years ago about the best way of handling this problem when it arose. Briquettes are put into a specially designed holder in the first tender and all water from either tender gets treated before it reaches the boiler.

When I bought 4472 in 1963, she had a conventional tender. Back in 1928, however, she had been the first locomotive in the world to be equipped with a corridor tender, the purpose of which was to enable engine crews to be changed on the non-stop runs en route between London and Edinburgh. I arranged at the time of purchase to "swop" tenders with A4 No. 60034, and that locomotive spent its last days with 4472's post-war non-corridor tender, while 4472 runs to this day with the one off that A4.

Although it has been rare for train crews to use the corridor for changing over since 4472 became a privately-owned locomotive, the corridor proved so useful in so many ways that when a second tender became a necessity I was determined to get another one of the same variety. Very few were ever built—only about a dozen, I think—and by early 1966, when I wanted to make the further purchase, no corridor tender in a runable state was available. However, A4 60009 *Union of South Africa* had by this time been virtually withdrawn from service, and was standing at Aberdeen as a spare engine for the summer Glasgow-Aberdeen services of that year. She had a corridor tender, but it was in a very poor way and therefore going

comparatively cheap. Although I was able to buy the tender for under £1,000, a further £5,000 had to be spent before it had been converted to its present state and made safe to run at 80 mph between the conventional tender and the train.

4472 first emerged from Doncaster with two tenders on October 3, 1966. It was a dreadfully wet and depressing day and not at all the sort one would have chosen for a unique outing of this sort. We ran light engine to Barkstone and back, using the north and south curves to turn, and running at no more than about 40 mph on the outward leg. All seemed to be well when we made our "stop and examine" scheduled halt adjacent to Barkstone East box and we returned to Doncaster at a nice steady 60 mph. No modifications of any sort seemed to be necessary and only five days later we tried out the second tender on a working train.

This was from Lincoln to Blackpool and again everything went without a hitch. Coming back at night, however, there was some confusion about just how much water we really had and we stopped in the middle of nowhere to find out. There was a further occasion in the early days of the second tender when an inspector on the engine was convinced the water supply was nearly exhausted and the train was stopped on the avoiding line at Bedford. Here, 4472 was uncoupled and went puffing off into the night in search of an alleged sole surviving water column in that area, leaving a 12-coach train packed with over 700 baffled passengers looking decidedly worried.

Incredibly, we located a water column (thanks to a very observant Midland driver) and eventually collected our train again and continued to St. Pancras, but we were very late and I felt acutely embarrassed about the whole thing.

Now, of course, the second tender is an animal with which I and the "regulars" are quite familiar. It can be isolated from the first tender and used purely as a reserve tank, or the cocks between the two tenders can be kept open as though one is, in effect, running on one 11,000-gallon tender. The range this gives one varies according to the load and the way the engine is being worked, but with a seven-coach train, no stopping, and economical working, the range would be nearly 300 miles. In practice, loads are usually of the order of 10 to 12 coaches and one tries to limit "dry" areas of running to about 150 miles. It can be an uncomfortable feeling to be low on water, with no assurance of any being available at one's destination, as sometimes happens.

Just as there were a few problems with the

second tender when it was new and unfamiliar, there have been problems with 4472 herself since the re-tubing was done early in 1969. It was early in 1965 that the last major boiler work had been carried out on the engine, and at that time running-in turns could be found in the shape of early morning newspaper trains and the like. In the old days, it was not uncommon for a main-line express passenger locomotive like *Flying Scotsman* to work on local passenger trains, parcels trains or even fast freight before undertaking top passenger duties again and as much as 3,000 miles often elapsed before this happened. No such arrangements were possible in 1969 and apart from one journey of 120 miles which was run under "light engine" conditions (the engine, one tender and one coach) no running of any kind was made until 4472 started working special excursions again. 4472 had never before worked "specials" in the month of February and the less said about the organisers' feelings on the subject the better. On the very first run of all the buffet car froze up overnight and a substitute vehicle was sent to go in its place. The train in which this alternative buffet car was being worked ran so late that 4472 and her train (with 679 schoolchildren on board) did not start until nearly an hour and a half after the advertised departure time.

The pattern seemed to continue in this way with extraordinary delays occurring that had nothing to do with the engine—an example—one Saturday morning the light engine working from Hornsey to St. Pancras (allowance, under $1\frac{1}{2}$ hours) took no less than $3\frac{3}{4}$ hours! This entailed a late start of nearly an hour. The one bright spot was a run from New Southgate and Welwyn Garden City to York, when 4472 romped along so merrily that she was no less than 22 minutes ahead of time passing Retford. Not surprisingly, this was too good to last and there were bad delays after that, but even so the arrival at York was some seven minutes early. But repairs to various steam joints had to be made unexpectedly on 4472 herself and one leg of two consecutive trips had to be diesel-hauled while the work was being done, while on another occasion a diesel had to be coupled on to the front of 4472 to give assistance in the last stages of the journey.

These are the sort of hazards one must learn to live with if one is going to be a "loner". There is nothing more exhilarating than riding on the footplate of one's own steam locomotive when all is going well, and nothing more nerve-racking than being in the same position when there is a spot of trouble. Thanks to the corridor tenders one can always go and tell the passengers in the train exactly what is going on, but this does not overcome the problem of keeping the lineside crowds informed. Although no professional public relations or publicity firm has been employed so far as 4472 is concerned since the spring of 1968, people invariably seem to know when she's about. Particularly since the BBC's TV film documentary about the 40th anniversary non-stop run (page 43) they turn out in ever increasing numbers. Great stuff, as I say, when all is going well.

What of the future? 1972 will be the first year when no main-line steam will be seen at all in Britain, unless there is a change of policy in high places. This seems improbable, but of course one never knows. If the ban does become absolute 4472 may well head for the mainland of Europe, but at this stage there are so many imponderables that it would be a rash man indeed who would try to make a firm forecast. If December 31, 1971 does turn out to be the end of the line for 4472, there will surely be many thousands who will wish her a peaceful retirement in the happy shunting grounds where all good steam engines go eventually. And has one railway locomotive ever brought more happiness, not just to her lucky owner but to countless thousands, old and young, male and female, throughout the main (and not so main) lines of British Railways?

▶ Youthful admirer.   [E. N. Kneale

▼ Last run by No. 60103 *Flying Scotsman* in BR service, with the 1.15 pm Kings Cross–Leeds on January 14, 1963.   [D. L. Percival

Kings Cross–Edinburgh Non-Stop

TREVOR BAILEY

IT WAS the most natural thing in the world that Alan Pegler should buy 4472, for there can never have been a more dedicated Gresley Pacific enthusiast. Though I knew him at school, it was not until undergraduate days that he first preached the LNER gospel to me. On my arrival in my rooms as a freshman, I was greeted by a note advising me that Alan was in residence in lodgings at 36, Jesus Lane. From then on Cambridge Station and its trains became our principal recreational target.

Up to then, I had never wandered far or for long from the Great Western territories on which I had been brought up. Other railways existed, in a rather remote way, and provided unfamiliar sights and sounds, but the GW was "home" and vastly superior in all departments withal. Now I was to have my eyes opened.

We spent a great deal of time at various lineside vantage points photographing trains, our most favoured spot being Sandy, which was easily reached by LMS cheaply and in a short time. Here it was that I saw my first streamliner in the shape of an A4 at the head of the down "Coronation" overtaking our LMS diesel unit on the parallel track approaching Sandy station. It was the beginning of a long and intimate acquaintance with the LNER, which lasted through the war and right up to the end of steam; in those far-off days, the A1s and A3s were apple-green and the A4s were blue, and you could really see the paint. We have become so used to 4472 as a unique institution to-day that it is easy to forget that there were well over a hundred Gresley Pacifics at work then.

We used to see 4472 occasionally, though as far as I can recall, the only trip I ever had behind her prior to 1963 was on an up express on which I was travelling from Newark to Kings Cross during the

◀ *Flying Scotsman* on display at Chester in 1967.
[J. R. Carter

Next page: No. 4472 before the acquisition of its second tender. M. Pope

war, when she failed at Sandy, of all places. We had been running poorly all the way from Peterborough, and at the approach to Sandy we stopped, 4472 drew forward, a K3 was transferred from a freight which was waiting in the loop and 4472 backed down on to the freight. I never discovered the cause of this manoeuvre.

Towards the end of 1962, Alan told me that he was expecting to acquire 4472 shortly, so it came as no surprise to me when at the beginning of 1963 he told me that she was due for withdrawal on January 14 and that she was to be handed over to him on that day. The 1.15 pm Leeds was the train on which she was booked to make her last journey under BR ownership and I had set the day aside so that I could travel north on this great occasion.

Kings Cross Top Shed was a seething mass of press, cameras, tape-recorders and all the paraphernalia of publicity that morning, and the platforms at Kings Cross later were thronged with people to witness the departure. Such was the fame of *Flying Scotsman* and a foretaste of things to come.

I was present on the trials some weeks later, when the single chimney had been restored, and we ran on a perishing cold day from Doncaster to New England and back, but her first revenue-earning outing under private ownership was in April 1963, when she hauled the Festiniog Railway Special between Paddington and Ruabon. Here again, popular interest was phenomenal and staggeringly large crowds turned out to see her progress, notably at Snow Hill Station, Birmingham, where the platforms looked like the terraces of Wembley Stadium on Cup Final day.

For the next five years, 4472 became more and more a familiar part of the railway scene, and the lineside interest became more variable. On May 1, 1968, however, a most outstanding event took place.

Forty years earlier, the LNER, under the

inspired guidance of Sir Nigel Gresley, had introduced the first regular non-stop daily service between Kings Cross and Edinburgh, and it had long been Alan's ambition to do a repeat performance on the actual anniversary day. The problems, however, were immense and thoroughly daunting. Not least of them was the fact that few people really wanted the run to take place, and the official climate at that time was so unfavourable that some of those who did were afraid to say so.

Nevertheless, on the morning of May 1, 1968, on the fortieth anniversary of the first non-stop, a train of coaches stood at No. 10 platform at Kings Cross, with 4472 at the head, ready to go. It was an epic occasion, deemed by the BBC worthy of the attention of a vast assemblage of cameras, equipment and curiously-attired men and women who shuttled back and forth along the corridors with monotonous irregularity. It was also a

◀ Forty years on: No. 4472 waits to leave Kings Cross on its special non-stop run on May 1, 1968.
[E. M. Rowe

▼ For comparison No. 4472 leaves Kings Cross on May 1, 1928, the first of the regular non-stop runs to Edinburgh.

great occasion for the enthusiasts, who were able not only to relive a bit of the past but also enjoy the exciting uncertainty of a non-stop attempt. I recalled at the time that my last previous participation in a London–Edinburgh non-stop was in June, 1962, on the Stephenson Locomotive Society's "Aberdeen Flyer", when *Mallard's* attempt was frustrated by a freight with a hot box at Belford.

Excitement on May 1, 1968 was intense. There were many rumours flying around about the crew's doubts on water supplies and coal, though it seemed to me that the latter should not present any problem and in the event it did not. Water was clearly a little less certain. The troughs at Scrooby, Wiske Moor and Lucker were all still operative and 4472 had her second tender, so that, in theory at any rate, all should have been well—but that would have been too easy. BR had in fact, it was later discovered, reduced the water level in the troughs and forgotten to restore it before the run!

The actual journey was yet another triumphal progress. 4472 behaved immaculately in her best tradition. The thousands of linesiders had a great view, the filming helicopters and aircraft did their stuff for BBC2, and along the Northumberland coast RAF Whirlwinds flew a sort of guard of

honour at low level, one ahead and one on either side of the train. It was one of those gala occasions so rare now on rail, and an experience for which those of us who participated are eternally grateful to Alan, and his tenacity in achieving it in the teeth of impossible odds.

It had its moments of drama—first a broken rail north of Doncaster which necessitated a walking-pace crawl, but not a stop; and second a misunderstanding which nearly succeeded in defeating the non-stop attempt. At Berwick, a tanker of water was standing by in the goods yard in case of need and it had been agreed that we should be put "inside" at Berwick if necessary. In fact it was not necessary, but for some reason the signalman at Berwick got the message to put us "inside", and we had a "red" on the approach. This signal is visible from a long way off as the train comes down on the long curve from Tweedmouth, and we crept along waiting desperately for it to clear, presuming that there was something ahead. Once it became apparent that we were being put round the back at Berwick we pressed on, and finally wormed our way round the goods road with much whistling and fist-shaking and sighs of relief. But it was a tense few minutes!

There were no further difficulties and we ran into Waverley amidst the anticipated vast throng of sightseers, to be greeted by the pipes playing "Scotland the Brave" as they had welcomed 4472 forty years before. It was a thrilling moment and an emotional one, and I was acutely aware that here was something that we should never see again. As I watched the expression of wonderment on the face of a little boy sitting on his father's shoulder I thought how he would look back on this moment in years to come; and I consoled myself with the knowledge that I have 30 years of LNER memories to draw on.

4472 is shortly to leave these shores. Let us hope that she will return to a more favourable official climate, so that the sight and sound of her steam, and that of others, may continue to be enjoyed to the full.

▶ Front end.

▼ Oiling up at Weymouth.   [D. E. Canning

▼ No. 4472 eases over Wensum swing bridge, Norwich, while turning on the triangle during a visit on May 20, 1967.   [G. R. Mortimer

► Crowds at Kings Cross before the start of the "Michaelangelo" tour in May 1966.   [P. Hocquard

▲ No. 4472 storms up the last stage of the climb to Ais Gill on the Midland–Carlisle main line with "The Moorlands" tour in October 1968.   [David Percival

▶ Reflections on spit and polish at Norwich, May 1967.
[P. Hocquard

▲ Another shot of "The Moorlands" railtour in October 1968 as No. 4472 surmounts the climb out of Wigan at Boars Head Junction. [Robert J. Clarke

◄ Concentration. [P. Hocquard

► Since preservation No. 4472 has worked to many unfamiliar parts of the country; here *Flying Scotsman* eases round the curve approaching Staines with the returning "Farnborough Flyer" on September 10, 1966.
[G. D. King

▲ No. 4472 climbs from Hawick to Whitrope over Shankend Viaduct on the now closed Waverley route with a special from Darlington to Edinburgh on April 16, 1966. [Peter W. Robinson

▶ No. 4472 winds its way out of Newcastle Central with the "Scunthorpe Forum Flyer" for Edinburgh on June 25, 1967. [J. R. P. Hunt

▲ No. 4472 sweeps down over Chester-le-Street viaduct with a Doncaster–Edinburgh excursion in June 1967.   [M. Dunnett

▶ No. 4472 posed for J. R. Carter at Chester where it was displayed in July 1967.

▶ Loving admirers at Kings Cross.   [P. Hocquard

Next page: No. 4472 passes Postland Crossing in Lincolnshire with a Pullman special in 1965.
                                              [P. Hocquard

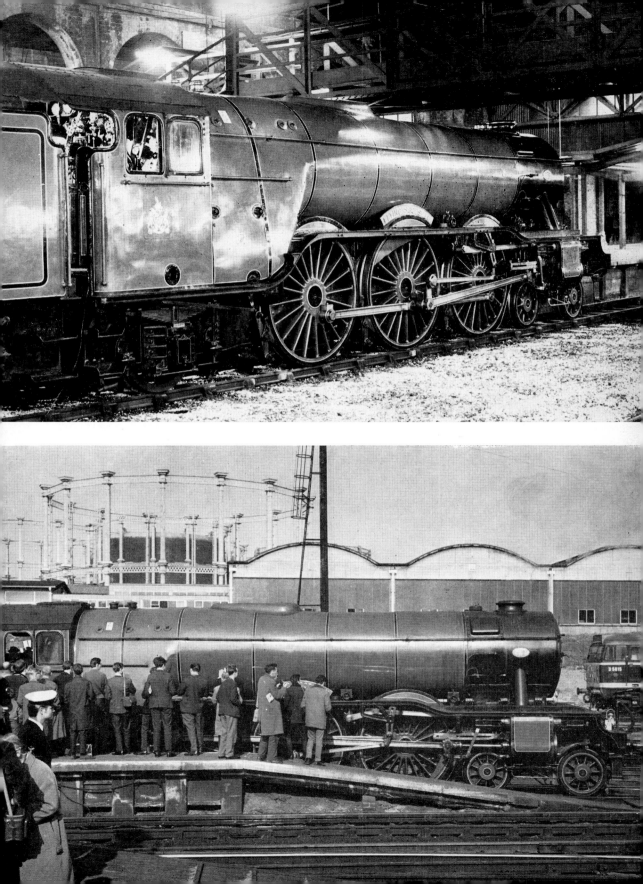

◀ On May 12, 1968, No. 4472 worked from Kings Cross to Norwich with the "Norfolk Enterprise" railtour seen here starting from Kings Cross.
[Eric Knight

▲ 4472 leaves Edinburgh Waverley with the return "Scunthorpe Forum Flyer" on June 25, 1967.
[John M. Boyes

◀ Ancient and modern; No. 4472 passes the South Hetton Colliery wagonway at Seaham Harbour with a Stockton–Edinburgh excursion on May 25, 1968.
[M. Dunnett

◄ Malcolm Dunnett's telephoto lens produces some interesting track patterns as 4472 eases over a tangle of rail outside Newcastle Central on May 10, 1969.

▼ Despite pouring rain 4472 draws the crowds for the Ian Allan "Brontë" special as it approaches Keighley on March 23, 1968. [B. Lister

▲ History—a famous locomotive, a famous bridge and a ferry; No. 4472 crosses the Forth Bridge on its way to Aberdeen on May 16, 1964. The ferry on the right has gone, for it has been replaced by the Forth roadbridge. [W. J. V. Anderson

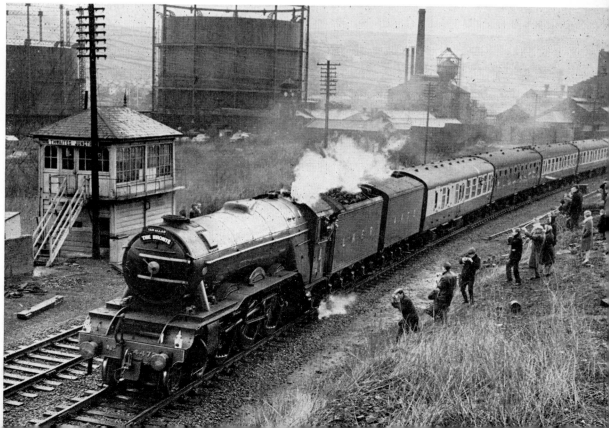

▲ 4472 in the lion's den, photographed crossing Wharncliffe viaduct near Hanwell with the Paddington–Cardiff "Panda Pullman" special on November 13, 1965. It was on a previous trip over rival Western Region metals that the engine failed during the journey, the cause looking suspiciously like sabotage.   [V. C. K. Allen

▶ When 4472 runs light and needs to propel its two tenders on running lines a guards brake van must be attached at the end for a look-out man to signal the driver. No. 4472 backs into Norwich in May 1967.
[P. Hocquard

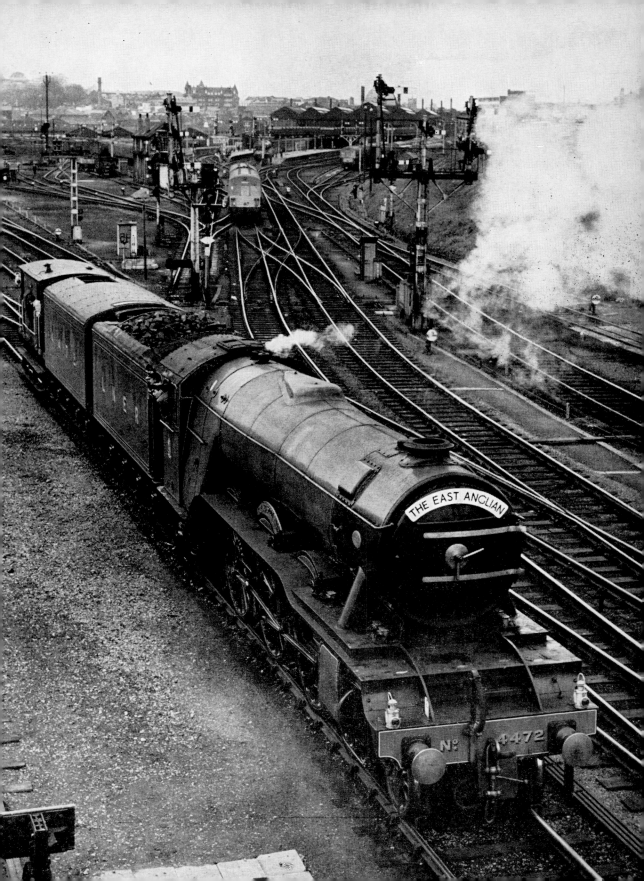

▲ Even when 4472 finally retires Pacifics of the same general design will still be running on the 15-in gauge Romney, Hythe & Dymchurch Railway in Kent. The RHDR 4-6-2s, built in 1925, were based on the Gresley 4-6-2s and as a tribute to Gresley one of the RHDR engines was photographed alongside 4472 at Kings Cross.

▼ No. 4472 leaves a smoke screen near Elstree on the very frosty morning of November 18, 1967 with an excursion from St Pancras.   [Graham S. Cocks